How To Become a Learning Machine

Quick Start Guide

I0482570

HTeBooks

Disclaimer

This book is designed to provide condensed information. It is not intended to reprint all the information that is otherwise available, but instead to complement, amplify and supplement other texts. You are urged to read all the available material, learn as much as possible and tailor the information to your individual needs.

Every effort has been made to make this book as complete and as accurate as possible. However, there may be mistakes, both typographical and in content. Therefore, this text should be used only as a general guide and not as the ultimate source of information. The purpose of this book is to educate.

The author or the publisher shall have neither liability nor responsibility to any person or entity regarding any loss or damage caused, or alleged to have been caused, directly or indirectly, by the information contained in this book.

Table of Contents

How Will This Book Help You?

This book aims to help one become a learning machine by defining what learning is, acknowledging the importance of learning and identifying and prevailing over the factors affecting it to promote learning in all aspects by increasing knowledge, cultivating skills and attaining wisdom.

"The illiterate of the 21st century will not be those who cannot read and write, but those who cannot learn, unlearn, and relearn." ~Alvin Toffler

What is Learning?

"All our knowledge begins with the senses, then proceeds to the understanding and ends with reason. There is nothing higher than reason."

- Immanuel Kant

Learning is defined as the act or process of gaining new knowledge, skills and attitudes or modifying or strengthening existing ones and integrating them as may be deemed useful to achieve one's goals.

Learning as a Process

Learning is not completed at one single time. It does not simply involve receiving information. It is a continuous process that is undergone by every individual who uses his reason to take in information and arrange them in such a way that they become understandable and useful.

Gaining New Knowledge, Skills and Attitudes

Knowledge, skills and attitudes may be acquired in various ways: through reading, observation, experience and teaching. Reading enables one to learn something through someone else's documented testimony or evidence of a subject he sought to explain through investigation, research or even experience. Observation enables the acquisition of personal knowledge about certain matters. Experience enables the acquisition of knowledge which may or may not have been taught. It is particularly important in learning skills, which must indeed be practiced to be learned. Knowledge acquired from being taught may be either enlightened or corruptible. Enlightened knowledge refers to that which requires explanation to be understood such as mathematical or scientific principles. On the other hand, corruptible knowledge refers to that which may be tainted with the teacher's biases upon being taught such as history and theology.

Modifying and Strengthening Existing Knowledge, Skills and Attitudes

Learning enables one to modify or strengthen his existing knowledge, skills and attitudes when he acknowledges and accepts new developments or revisions to that which he already knows. In simpler terms, this is what is known as adapting. It is particularly useful in finding better solutions to problems. An example of this is the development of vaccines to avoid being infected or afflicted with a serious illness.

Integrating

Finally, the key to learning lies in integration. Integration involves synthesizing all the information acquired through time and evaluating how they have been used in history or how they can be applied in a particular situation at present or even in the future.

In other words, integration entails the use of reason. Reason is defined as the ability to make sense of the information at hand by relating ideas to one another and understanding them with cause and effect (consequence), fact or fiction (truth) and good or bad (morality). It requires a conscious effort of validating facts and applying logic to justify or change existing beliefs and practices.

*Learning entails the use of reason.

The Importance of Learning

"Learning is the only thing the mind never exhausts, never fears, and never regrets."

- Leonardo da Vinci

Since the dawn of time, life has posed many challenges for man—from the allocation of limited resources and fear of the unknown to the consequences of failure. However, civilization continues to thrive as man persists in enduring and overcoming them by using the innate ability of his mind to learn.

Learning starts even before an individual is ready to go to school. While children and even babies are known to display an interest in learning, studies conducted within the latest decade have shown that an individual's motivation for learning declines upon reaching his teens. In fact, data from the National Research Council reveals that more than 40 per cent of high school students are constantly absent or withdrawn from school due to lack of motivation.

Nevertheless, such a condition is subject to change over time as research shows that more than 90 per cent of adults are more motivated to learn with various personal reasons such as to get a better paying job, boosting confidence, improving the quality of life and satisfaction.

While such reasons may encourage one's desire to learn, the importance of learning is simply that it allows individuals to freely stretch the limits of their humanity to find answers to their questions.

In other words, the universal and primary importance of learning is that through it, man is able to fulfill his essence as a thinking being and nothing can be greater than that.

*Learning is important because it enables man to fulfill his essence as a thinking being.

Factors Affecting Learning and how to Prevail Over Them

"The knowledge of all things is possible."

- Leonardo da Vinci

It is possible for man to know or learn everything he wants. However, learning is not easy. It may be affected by internal and external factors which must be dealt with so that true learning may ensue.

Internal Factors

Internal factors are those which originate from the individual's genetic make-up and intelligence. More specifically, it consists of his capacity to learn, his attitude towards learning and his motivation.

Capacity to Learn and Attitude towards Learning

An individual's capacity to learn and attitude towards learning often go hand in hand. While an individual's capacity to learn may be affected by his physical condition or traits, innate talent and intellect, the lack thereof does not necessarily preclude him from learning. It also doesn't mean that just because an individual is born with talent, he should not continue to learn to improve his craft. This is where an individual's attitude towards learning plays an important role. A major component of this attitude towards learning is having strength of will. If he is determined to learn and persists in doing so in spite of all the odds against him, then he shall most likely become a genius in his own right.

For instance, in spite of his musical talents, German composer and pianist Ludwig van Beethoven devoted his time to studying and learning under the direction of Classical composer Franz Joseph Haydn before setting out to become a composer. Although he became deaf by the age of 26, he was yet able to continue producing great works such as his famous masterpiece, The Ninth Symphony.

Similarly, American author Helen Keller, who became deaf and blind due to an illness before reaching the age of two, persisted in learning until she graduated cum laude with her Bachelor of Arts degree in Radcliffe College. In spite of her physical disabilities, she was also able to write several essays and twelve books which were eventually published.

On a different note, contrary to the impression his fans have of him, basketball star Michael Jordan likewise had to learn how to perfect his jump shot to become a legend in spite of his phenomenal athletic skills and complementary physical attributes, as revealed by his longstanding coach, Phil Jackson.

Another component of an individual's attitude towards learning also requires him to have an open mind. This involves challenging ideas before accepting them and accepting them only if they have not yet been displaced by new discoveries or innovative ideas.

An example of this—though considered controversial in other places around the world--is learning without any religious biases. It is difficult to learn many things about life in general if one has to start with the assumption that everything comes from God. Another example is the acceptance of the flat earth model which was held from the classical to the Hellenistic periods until a new idea of the Earth as a sphere emerged with Pythagoras until it was proven by Christopher Columbus in his voyage around the earth.

Motivation

Unless a person acknowledges and accepts his essence as a thinking being as the primary motivation for learning, he is only capable of obtaining provisional knowledge which can fade through time after the particular motivation for learning has been attained. Accepting one's essence as a thinking being enables the pursuit of true learning: learning for learning's sake.

External Factors

External factors are those which are usually beyond the control of the individual. They include the availability of resources, the source of learning, the cost of learning and the environmental conditions.

Availability of Resources

In reality, everything can be considered a resource for learning. However, the availability of resources for specific learning may be limited and quite costly. For instance, the individual's financial resources may not be sufficient to cover the cost of learning a particular course like Law which requires paying fees for enrollment in college and subsequently, Law School including the cost of materials such as law books and other incidental fees like transportation and lodging which can reach a minimum of approximately $30,000 to a maximum of more than $80,000 and may vary according to state.

Nevertheless, the lack of resources must not serve as an obstacle for individuals who truly want to learn as other options may be available. For instance, Abraham Lincoln, the 16th President of the United States, learned the law and became a lawyer without going to law school. He studied the law independently and obtained his license to practice law after passing an oral examination in front of a panel of lawyers in the Sangamon Country Court, Illinois. Although circumstances may have become more difficult in the past few decades, options for learning to become a lawyer are still available particularly in the states of Wyoming, California, Virginia, Vermont and Washington where self-study of the law together with apprenticeship can qualify an individual for the BAR exams and eventually practice law as an attorney.

Another valuable resource which people often fail to consider is time. It is limited to the present because the past no longer exists and the future is always unknown. Thus, an individual who wishes to learn must start now and even if the future holds no certainty, he may still set a reasonable time for everything he wants to learn. After all, time is only consumed in so far as events transpired before the present. The future still holds possibilities.

Source of Learning

One factor that affects the quality of learning is its source. It can either encourage true learning or serve as a hindrance to it. This is particularly true for subjects which are taught without the need for presenting empirical evidence. For instance, the lessons of history can be tainted with the teacher's ideological biases which can influence the students' minds. True learning is best obtained from firsthand experience or authoritative documentation such as books, academic journals or published texts by specialists on the given subject. On the other hand, true learning is impeded when one merely relies on opinionated articles or readily available or secondhand information particularly in the internet such as Wikipedia. In the words of the great Roman philosopher Marcus Tullius Cicero himself, "The authority of those who teach is often an obstacle to those who want to learn."

Environment

The environment largely contributes to an individual's ability to learn. It consists of the areas in which he moves such as the home, school and neighborhood as well as the city, state or country where he belongs.

Home

The home is one's primary place of learning. From his earliest motor and cognitive skills to his first interpersonal relationships as well as academic pursuits, the home has served as his first school. Thus, an atmosphere conducive for learning must be maintained always. This includes the encouragement and support of family members, the neatness and orderliness of study areas as well as freedom from noise and other distractions.

School

An individual usually pursues more specific areas of study in school. It can inspire him to pursue higher learning or discourage him from further learning depending on the following elements: teaching style, system of assessment, extracurricular activities and pressure groups.

Teaching Style

Teaching style can greatly affect an individual's learning as it refers to the manner in which lessons are taught. Studies have shown that interactive teaching styles are more effective than traditional information transfer through lectures as they produce better understanding and higher grades.

System of Assessment

Grades are based on the system of assessment which may vary for every teacher. However, subjective criteria for evaluation should be avoided to measure actual learning with more accuracy. Moreover, the system of assessment must also be able to measure how much the student has learned and not just provide a basis for grades. In other words, tests must be formulated to generate critical thinking based on the given information while projects and other requirements must be an application of relevant theories, principles or ideas. For instance, history tests must not consist solely of identification of names and dates but more importantly, of reasons, causes and effects. Similarly, math and science projects should present more challenges by encouraging new ideas in the application of mathematical and scientific knowledge.

Extracurricular Activities

Learning is not limited to the intellect. The existence of extracurricular activities such as intramurals, school fairs, dances, homecomings, competitions and other organizations encourages an individual's complete learning as he is allowed to explore other aspects of his being.

Pressure groups

While the presence of pressure groups such as bullies, junkies, frat men, sorority girls, racists or snooty cliques can discourage an individual from learning in school, they can, on the other hand, serve as competition and push the strong-willed to learn more or serve as subjects to individuals who want to learn about human behavior.

Neighborhood

An individual's neighborhood can either function as his prison cell or his laboratory, depending on his desire to learn. For instance, a neighborhood run by goons or drug dealers can prevent him from exploring his surroundings due to the threats he may come across. On the other hand, a peaceful and secure neighborhood can function as his laboratory where he is free to explore his surroundings and interact with his neighbors healthily.

City, State or Country

Finally, an individual's learning can also be affected by the larger area where he belongs. More specifically, some cities have strict regulations such as zoning laws which may prohibit certain activities on particular lots while some countries which continue to discriminate against race and gender prohibit the education of certain groups. For instance, in Middle Eastern countries like Kuwait and Oman, education is biased in favor of male in students as female students are required to obtain higher averages to be able admitted in certain courses like engineering as well as in Saudi Arabia where more classes and courses are made available to men than to women.

Democratic countries such as the United States, on the other hand, provide greater learning opportunities for all through government-funded scholarships, grants and other incentives. Similarly, companies and non-governmental institutions create educational opportunities as well.

Considerably, nothing can prevent an individual from learning except himself.

Prevailing over these factors will enable him to pursue true learning by increasing his knowledge, cultivating his skills and attaining wisdom.

*The propensity to overcome obstacles is directly proportional to one's desire for learning.

Increasing Knowledge

"To know what you know and what you do not know, that is true knowledge."

- Confucius

Knowledge is defined as information consisting of facts or theories pertaining to a certain subject. In a more general context, it is the sum of all truths and principles acquired and accumulated through time and upheld by humanity. It may pertain to truths which must yet be established or those which have already been ascertained or at least, have been accepted as true.

Learning truths which must yet be established

There are two ways of generating knowledge which remains to be established: through rationalism and empiricism. Rationalism makes use of innate ideas, logic and deductive reasoning which relies on premises to arrive at a definite conclusion. On the other hand, empiricism involves the use of observation and inductive reasoning which only requires strong evidence instead of absolute proof as the basis for the conclusion.

Knowledge through Rationalism

Rationalism presupposes that man is born with innate ideas which, according to philosophers like Plato, can explain why some individuals are naturally better at performing or resolving some tasks than others are in spite of the similarity of experiences. It also acknowledges reason as the major cause of knowledge in contrast with the senses which, according to rationalists like Descartes, can only give opinions since they can be deceived. Thus, conclusions can be proven with certainty using rationalism. An example of this is Descarte's attempt to prove the existence of God where he starts with the premise that he has an idea of a perfect substance but since he is not a perfect substance, a perfect substance like God must exist because only perfection is capable of creating perfection.

Knowledge through Empiricism

Empiricism, on the other hand, presumes that knowledge originates from perception. More specifically, philosopher John Locke explains that simple ideas are based on perception or observation of physical qualities like shape or color while complex ideas are formed by combining simple ideas. Empiricists reject innate ideas as the source of knowledge because individuals do not demonstrate knowledge at birth or in the early stages of their life as in childhood, where children must learn how to talk and walk. Thus, empiricists believe that things cannot be proven conclusively as no one can be certain that the thing remains the same once the individual stops perceiving it. In other words, the mind is likened to a blank slate upon which experience imparts knowledge in all aspects—intelligence, social and emotional behavior.

Debating on their acceptability is quite useless since there is absolutely no conflict as both ways can be applied in learning. Rationalism may be used to learn about things which observation cannot answer such as the existence of God while empiricism may be used to learn about things which must rely on observation to be applied effectively as in scientific studies on the effects of medicine, etc.

Learning truths which have already been ascertained or accepted as true

Rationalism and empiricism are generally used in obtaining knowledge which has not yet been accepted as true. However, for facts which have already been ascertained or accepted as true, one may employ one or more learning styles to aid in his absorption of knowledge. These learning styles can be generally divided into two: individual or social learning.

Individual learning

Individual learning style presumes one's preference for self-study. The desire to work alone usually enables one to learn at his ideal pace and align learning objectives with personal values and standards.

Individual learning further enables one to choose freely among the following learning styles to suit his needs: visual learning, auditory learning, physical learning and logical or mathematical learning.

Visual learning

This learning style generally starts with looking at an entire system, the whole or the "big picture" before probing into the details. It makes use of images such as photos, drawings or other visual aids like tables, graphs and charts instead of words in learning. It may also use imagination or photographic memory and color-coding of notes. This style is recommended for learning how to write foreign words which require the use of characters such as Chinese, Japanese or Korean, memorizing geographic locations and descriptions or legal cases involving family relations or crime.

Auditory Learning

Auditory learning makes use of any kind of sound whether used as a background for studying or to facilitate association or recall. For instance, using classical music, particularly that of Mozart as a background for studying, has been shown in studies conducted at Stanford University to have beneficial effects including the reduction of learning time, the decrease in errors and the improvement of clarity. On the other hand, association and recall of information may be enhanced by developing them into rhymes or incorporating them in rhythmic beats and popular jingles. This also includes recording one's voice or orally repeating important points which can help strengthen memory. This type of learning is particularly useful for learning how to speak a foreign language.

Physical learning

Physical learning entails field work or active participation by making use of physical objects to help demonstrate theories which may be difficult to understand. For instance, using common tools like a nutcracker or tweezers to demonstrate laws of physics may help in understanding terms such as effort, fulcrum and resistance more easily. Similarly, toys like cubes and balls or origami creations may also be used to explain geometric theories like lines, planes, spheres and space. It may also mean learning while doing a physical activity such as jogging, going back and forth across the room or eating.

Logical or Mathematical Learning

Logical or mathematical learning generally entails using specific principles in the mathematical system to understand how formulas were derived to be able to solve mathematical problems more easily in contrast to memorization without reason, which can produce disastrous results if there is a mental block. An example would be using theorems to prove congruence in geometry and properties of multiplication, addition and equality to solve for unknown variables in algebra.

Social Learning

This type of learning is for individuals who prefer to learn from others in groups through activities like sharing, role playing, constructive argumentation or debates.

With all the learning styles available, man has no excuse to remain ignorant.

*There are many ways to gain knowledge.

Cultivating Skills

"For the things we have to learn before we can do them, we learn by doing them."

- Aristotle

To become a learning genius , one must not confine himself to the pursuit of knowledge. Whether born as or developed into, geniuses are exceptional at different forms of learning. As shown in the previous chapter, they can successfully use their reason to discover new knowledge or modify accepted truths. In terms of skills, learning geniuses can either discover and unleash their skills or establish themselves as creative geniuses in the performance of their skills.

A skill is defined as the ability to perform physical tasks with a certain degree of aptitude. They may either be general or specific.

General Skills

General skills are those which are transferrable or applicable to various activities or functions in all sectors—whether household, commercial or financial, industrial, educational or social. They include leadership, organization, budget administration, time management and communication.

Specific Skills

Specific skills, on the other hand, are those which are functional or effective only for a particular task such as auditing skills for an accountant, culinary skills for a chef or hair cutting and coloring skills for hairdressers.

Like knowledge, skills may either be learned or enhanced. In both cases, training, practice and persistence are required.

Training

Training is defined as the process of acquiring certain competencies from professionals or experts in order to achieve a higher standard of proficiency. It may be undertaken through formal lessons for talents such as singing, dancing and playing the piano or apprenticeships for technical skills for electricians and auto mechanics.

Practice

Practice entails the repeated performance of specific exercises designed to increase proficiency. In order to obtain the best results, one must first take note of his mistakes and avoid committing them again. Moreover, he must not reduce the act of rehearsing into a mere routine. Instead, he must perform passionately and seek to surpass each performance with a challenge to go beyond perfection. After all, one can find himself in losing himself.

Persistence

Persistence is a quality which enables one to continue doing something in spite of some difficulties he may encounter. For instance, although Van Gogh began drawing in his childhood until he decided to become an artist, he produced a multitude of sketches in order to improve his talent for years before he finally completed his best art works in the remaining years of his life. Although it took more than a decade for his works to be recognized, he continued to strive for perfection.

Similarly, four-time Grammy Award winner Taylor Swift, who started writing songs when she was five, persisted in writing and singing her music in spite of being mistreated by fellow students in school and unfairly judged by critics until she was finally recognized by Sony Music publishing and became the star that she is.

Talent without persistence can go unrecognized.

*One can be born with talent and skill but it is in persistence that he can achieve greatness.

Attaining Wisdom

"Wisdom is not a product of schooling but of the lifelong attempt to acquire it."

- Albert Einstein

More than knowledge and skills, the ultimate goal of a learning genius is to acquire wisdom. Wisdom is defined as the ability to incorporate knowledge, awareness, experience, retrospection and understanding in order to act or make a choice. As such, it cannot be taught or learned in school. It is the result of one's assessment of his experiences where he recognizes his mistakes and resolves to avoid them in future instances.

It requires knowledge relevant to the given situation in order to evaluate his predicament and determine what can be done, awareness of what he is faced with (resources, alternatives and advantages or disadvantages), experience and retrospection in order to enable him to make the right judgment and understanding in order to be able to deal with the possible consequences of his choice. In other words, it is knowing exactly what to say or do in any given situation and being ready to accept the consequences of one's actions.

Thus, wisdom has four components: the ability to accept the limits of one's knowledge, the ability to find the middle ground, the ability to exercise objectivity and the ability to apply foresight.

Accepting the limits of one's knowledge

In order to make a good decision, one must turn to his own knowledge involving the issue at hand. However, he must learn to admit when his knowledge is insufficient to allow him to make the correct decision. In such cases, he may either refer to other sources or seek counsel from qualified authorities before making a decision.

Finding the Middle Ground

Finding the middle ground entails the ability to compromise. It involves reaching an agreement where all parties forfeit individual benefits in favor of a mutually advantageous arrangement. This is particularly useful in situations requiring negotiations such as collective bargaining agreements, business transactions or even a hostage crisis.

Exercising Objectivity

In order to arrive at a compromise, one must necessarily exercise objectivity and weigh all matters from each party's respective standpoints. It is only by doing so that a mutually beneficial arrangement can be reached. Furthermore, objectivity enables one to think clearly and use his reason more effectively as it will not be clouded with subjective biases. This is best exemplified in judicial pronouncements of acquittal or conviction as well as matters pertaining to morality.

Applying Foresight

Foresight is the ability to foresee all possible outcomes of a certain course of action. It allows the individual to choose the best course of action out of all possible actions and enables him to accept the consequences that may arise therefrom, knowing that the outcome was the least disadvantageous result among the only courses of action available at that time. This may be applied in times of financial crisis when one is faced with various alternatives for producing funds. For instance, choosing to sell one's assets instead of contracting an interest-generating loan would be the less disadvantageous for the individual as his liabilities will not increase.

All in all, wisdom guides man in all his judgments. Thus, it is the greatest purpose of learning.

*The attainment of wisdom is the ultimate goal of learning.

Become a Learning Genius

"Change is the end result of all true learning."

- Leo Buscaglia

While one might argue that there are truths which cannot be changed like the law of gravity or that a routinely life does not enable the discovery of anything new, everyone nevertheless learns something new everyday. This is because everyday is a different day. It is not yesterday.

A learning genius never runs out of things to learn for he knows that there are still other things which he does not know and what he knows today might not be the same tomorrow or if not, after an extended period of time. For instance, the geocentric model of the universe espoused by philosophers like Aristotle and Ptolemy which ancient civilizations accepted as true for hundreds of years was later on replaced with the model of heliocentrism as advocated by Nicolaus Copernicus, Galileo Galilei and Johannes Kepler, which did not become popular until the 16th century.

Similarly, the theory of spontaneous generation promoted by philosophers like Anaximander, Hippolytus, Aristotle and Anaxagoras which provides that life could be produced from nothing (as in the case of maggots coming out of biodegradable objects like animal carcasses or rotting fruit) was generally held as true for centuries and was proven wrong only after the 1700s with the use of the scientific method where such theories were tested. More specifically, they were immediately proven wrong when microbiologist Louis Pasteur used experimentation to show that maggots did not appear on meat which was sealed in a container and were instead produced by airborne microorganisms as seen through the microscope which was newly invented at that time. To wit, new inventions and further experimentation can lead to new learning which can refute and modify existing truths.

As long as there is life, everyone continues to learn by observation and by experience. Some choose to continue to improve their skills and strive to be better than yesterday while some choose to give up. Nevertheless, each choice made by an individual is a learning opportunity for another. Every question generates an answer and each answer is a new learning for the inquisitive mind. Only the mind can challenge what it already knows.

*A learning genius, therefore, never ceases to use his reason in all things, at all times.

Key Points

*Learning entails the use of reason.

*Learning is important because it enables man to fulfill his essence as a thinking being.

*The propensity to overcome obstacles is directly proportional to one's desire for learning.

*There are many ways to gain knowledge.

*One can be born with talent and skill but it is in persistence that he can achieve greatness.

*The attainment of wisdom is the ultimate goal of learning.

*A learning genius, therefore, never ceases to use his reason in all things, at all times.